Arizona Bucket List Adventure Guide & Journal

Explore The Natural Wonders & Log Your Experience!

Bridge Press

Bridge Press
dp@purplelink.org

Please consider writing a review!
Just visit: purplelink.org/review

ISBN: 978-1-955149-13-6

FREE BONUS

Find Out 31 Incredible Places You Can Visit
Next! Just Go To:

purplelink.org/travel

Table of Contents:

How to Use This Book

Welcome to your very own adventure guide to exploring the natural wonders of the state of Arizona. Not only does this book lay out the most wonderful places to visit and sights to see in the vast state, but it also serves as a journal so you can record your experience.

Adventure Guide
Sorted by region, this guide offers 50 amazing wonders of nature found in Arizona for you to go see and explore. These can be visited in any order, and this book will help keep track of where you've been and where to look forward to going next.

Each portion describes the area or place, what to look for, how to get there, and what you may need to bring along. A map is also included so you can map out your destinations.

Journal Your Experience
Following each location description is a fillable journal page for you. During or after your visit, you can jot down in the journal portion significant sights encountered, events confronted, people involved, and memories you gained while on your adventure. This will add even more value to your experience and keep a record of your time spent witnessing the greatest wonders of Arizona.

GPS Coordinates and Codes
As you can imagine, not all of the locations in this book have a physical address. Fortunately, some of our listed wonders are either located within a national park or reserve or are near a city, town, or place of business. For those that are not associated with a specific location, it is easiest to map it using GPS coordinates.

Luckily, Google has a system of codes that converts the coordinates into pin-drop locations that Google Maps is able to interpret and navigate.

Each adventure in this guide will include the GPS coordinates along with general directions on how to find the location and Google Plus codes whenever possible.

How to find a location using Google Plus:

1. Open Google Maps on your device.
2. In the search bar, type the Google Plus code as it is printed on the page.
3. Once the pin is located, you can tap on "Directions" for step-by-step navigation.

It is important that you are prepared for poor cell signals. It is recommended to route your location and ensure that the directions are accessible offline. Depending on your device and the distance of some locations, you may need to travel with a backup battery source.

About Arizona

Arizona is the 48th state in the United States, and its unique natural landscape, with locations such as the Grand Canyon, Monument Valley, and Havasu Falls, has been a staple of state history. Major cities of Phoenix, Tucson, and Scottsdale allow for a "home base" for those wanting to explore the wonders of the state.

Before statehood, the state was home to Native Americans who lived in the area for thousands of years. In the modern-day, the Navajo and Tohono O'odham Nations are the two largest reservations in the United States. The history and influence of the region's indigenous people can be seen around the state, with historical landmarks allowing for further education. The Mesa Verde are some of the best-preserved pueblos (villages) in North America. Dating nearly a millennium old, created around 1190, these homes give an insight into the Pueblo people's world.

The Colorado River's power has been the life force of the state for nearly 70 million years. Carving out the landscape of the northern region, including the famed Grand Canyon, the river's strength even supplies the surrounding states with water and power due to the Hoover Dam. The dam also protects Arizona, California, and Nevada from flooding that can occur during a wet season in the Colorado River.

The rich history of Arizona and its unique landscape has brought visitors for hundreds of years to the region. With the continued support of the national parks, these protected regions can be enjoyed for hundreds of more years.

Landscape and Climate

The state has multiple landscapes and climates, with the north and south regions of the state having nearly opposite landscapes and climates. Both regions have their own plants and animals that call the area home and have been there for hundreds of years. There are three geographical regions of the state: The Basin and Range (south), Transition Zone (middle), and Colorado Plateau (north).

The southern region of the state has a desert climate within the Basin and Range region. There is extreme heat in summers, many days with a temperature above 100°F (37.8°C), and mild temperatures in the winter around 50°F (10°C). This region of the state receives little rainfall during the year, furthering the intense climate. To adapt to the climate, many of the native plants are cacti. There is a vast number in the region, and some flower while others grow multiple feet tall.

The Colorado Plateau that encompasses the northern region of the state has a less extreme climate, allowing for the growth of forests housing pine trees. The largest ponderosa pine trees in the world are located within Arizona! With the Colorado Plateau running across the region, mountains and canyons have formed in the areas. During the winter, this region even experiences snow nearly 40 inches in some areas, allowing for ski resorts to operate. The Colorado River runs through the northwest area of the state and is the cause of the Grand Canyon! The Hoover Dam is also located on the border of Arizona and Nevada.

The state's two major geographic regions have created two vastly different landscapes and climates within a small area. Visitors to the state can experience different scenic experiences without needing to travel far!

Grand Canyon

Located within the state of Arizona, the Grand Canyon has been a place to visit for generations. Given the prestigious title as one of the Seven Natural Wonders of the World, it has an estimated 5.9 million visitors each year, making this park the most popular national park in the United States. The first outside visitors exploring the region around 1540 were the Spanish, with hopes of finding a fictional city of gold. Carved out by the Colorado River over millions of years, some scientists believe the Canyon is nearly 70 million years old. The Canyon's unique rock formations and size seem "out of this world" and can actually be seen from space! The deepest point of the Canyon is 6,000 feet, and it is 18 miles across at the widest section. The Canyon is so large that it contains five ecosystems: three types of forests (boreal, ponderosa pine, and pinyon-juniper woodlands) and two types of desert systems (desert scrub and desert). The deep canyons have allowed geologists to study and learn about the rock formations, offering a better understanding of the Earth and its history. Besides studying the rocks, anthropologists have been studying artifices of human villages found in the region. Humans have lived in and around the Grand Canyon for over 10,500 years since the last Ice Age.

Best time to visit:
March to May
September to November
Pass/Permit/Fees:
$35 Vehicle Permit (Day Pass) or $80 Annual National Park Pass
Closest city or town:
Tusayan, Arizona
How to get there:
Fly into Las Vegas, Salt Lake City, or Phoenix, and rent a car to drive to the park. There are also shuttles that will take visitors from Phoenix to the park.
GPS Coordinates:
36.0544° N, 112.1401° W
Did You Know?
The Grand Canyon is bigger than the state of Rhode Island!

Journal:

Date(s) Visited:

Weather conditions:

Who you were with:

Nature observations:

Special memories:

Sedona

This small town located near Flagstaff is home to vast natural rock formations. Visitors travel to Sedona to see the red rock mountains and hike along trails that offer unique and vast views of the region. Bell Rock, Cathedral Rock, Devil's Bridge, and many more natural wonders have kept hikers coming back for years to explore. The Red Rock Scenic Byway might be the most beautiful road you'll ever drive on. Highway 179 is the best way to drive from Sedona to Phoenix, and the towering red rocks line the drive for the entire seven miles. Nicknamed "a museum without walls," there are many locations to explore along the highway. Popular areas to visit on the highway are Bell Rock, Coconino National Forest, and the Village of Oak Creek. Many visitors travel to Sedona to experience vortices. For thousands of years, people have used this area as a place for spiritual healing. Four main vortices in Sedona are Airport Mesa, Cathedral Rock, Bell Rock, and Boynton Canyon. Many people practice yoga and other forms of meditation within these areas to experience the vortices' force. Sedona is surrounded by 1.8 million acres of national forest land, making this an ideal location for any outdoor fan.

Best time to visit:
March to May, October to November
Pass/Permit/Fees:
None, permits might be needed for certain hiking trails
Closest city or town:
Flagstaff, Arizona
How to get there:
Fly into Flagstaff or Phoenix airport and rent a car to drive to Sedona. There are also shuttles that transport from Phoenix to Sedona.
GPS Coordinates:
34° 51' 35.63" N, -111° 47' 21.12" W
Did You Know?
The McDonald's located in Sedona is the only place in the world to have green arches, rather than the standard yellow! This was done to not distract from the natural color of the landscape.

Journal:

Date(s) Visited:

Weather conditions:

Who you were with:

Nature observations:

Special memories:

Monument Valley

Monument Valley, or *Tsé Bii' Ndzisgaii* in Navajo, which translates to valley of rocks, is made up of sandstone buttes, mesas, and cliffs rock formations. These mammoth buttes stand up over 1,000 feet on the desert floor. Without any nearby mountains or hills, these buttes seem to be out of place. The valley has multiple hiking trails and the option to drive your car on a self-guided tour around the most popular spots. Over 50 million years of natural erosion by wind and water resulted in the height of the buttes. Geologists have been able to study the region's four rock formations of Organ Rock Shale, De Chelly Sandstone, Moenkopi, and Shinarump. The bright red color of the iron oxide leaves the valley with a unique color scheme. The valley and buttes have been inhabited by people since AD 1300 – the Anasazi people. The Navajo people would later inhabit this region and still remain there today! Monument Valley is located within the Navajo Nation Reservation and encompasses nearly 92,000 acres of land. The region is not a national park but rather a Navajo Tribal Park! It was not until the 1930s that this location became famous due to a John Ford film. After the popularity of the movie, people started to travel and explore the region! It's now iconic and has thousands of visitors each year.

Best time to visit:
April to May, September to October
Pass/Permit/Fees:
$10 per person or $20 per vehicle
Closest city or town:
Kayenta, Arizona or Mexican Hat, Utah
How to get there:
The closest airport is 320 miles away in Phoenix, Arizona. The only way to reach Monument Valley is via car.
GPS Coordinates:
36° 58' 59.99" N, -110° 05' 60.00" W
Did You Know?
Forest Gump was filmed along Route 163 – the iconic running scene showcased Monument Valley in the background.

Journal:

Date(s) Visited:

Weather
conditions:

Who you were with:

Nature observations:

Special memories:

Glen Canyon National Recreation Area

Glen Canyon National Recreation Area covers over 1.25 million acres of land in both Utah and Arizona. The area encompasses famed Lake Powell – the second-largest manmade lake in the United States. Like the Grand Canyon, the Colorado River carved out the region and left the unique shapes of rock formations. Lake Powell was created in 1963 due to the building of Glen Canyon Dam. The area is known for its exciting outdoor activities, from swimming and boating in Lake Powell to off-roading around the mountain region. One of the best ways to experience the natural wonders is by boat, canoe, or kayak! Deep caves and caverns were created over years of water and wind erosion, and these can be seen while on the water, offering a different view. Over millions of years, formation and erosion have created almost 40 layers of sedimentary rocks to view in areas. The deep red hues of the stones have brought photographers from around the world to capture the beauty. The park's size allows for multiple days to be spent exploring the natural landmarks and one-of-a-kind locations. Hikers travel to Glen Canyon to explore the national wonders, including Rainbow Bridge, Horseshoe Bend, and Reflection Canyon. Camping can be done on the Lake Powell shores or within the backcountry of the park.

Best time to visit:
March to May, September to November
Pass/Permit/Fees:
$14 for vehicles and $7 for bikes or motorcycles – the fee is good for seven consecutive days.
Closest city or town:
Page, Arizona
How to get there:
Glen Canyon can be reached by four different major highways (US Rt. 89, State Rt. 98, State Rt. 95, and State Rt. 276).
GPS Coordinates:
37° 23' 13.1604" N and 110° 50' 34.1628" W
Did You Know?
The dam that was created inside Glen Canyon is 583 feet high and 1,560 feet wide!

Journal:

Date(s) Visited:

Weather
conditions:

Who you were with:

Nature observations:

Special memories:

17

Spider Rock in Canyon de Chelly

Spider Rock is a 750-foot sandstone spire sacred to the Navajo and Hopi people. According to Navajo legend, Spider Grandmother resides on the larger of the two spires, and her helpers, the crows, live on the shorter of the two. According to myth, she takes the form of either a timeless woman or a common spider. Spider Grandmother worked with Tawa (the Sun God) to give the animals of the world souls. After this, they made humans after their likeness and sang them to life. Spider Grandmother taught men and women their roles and religious practices before dividing them into four groups and leading them to live in the Four Canyons. There are many legends regarding Spider Grandmother that are located both online and in books on Navajo and Hopi myths. However, since Spider Rock is considered a sacred location, visitors are prohibited. Its tower is visible from the South Rim Drive. Further on in this guide, there is more information available regarding Canyon de Chelly and its various ruins.

Best time to visit:
April to May, September to October
Pass/Permit/Fees:
No entrance fees
Closest city or town:
Chinle, Arizona
How to get there:
Taking the South Rim Drive will allow views of Spider Rock from the car. This is accessed by taking AZ 64 about 11 miles down and then following FR 310 another 1.3 miles to the trailhead. To visit the Canyon, visitors must travel with a park ranger or Navajo guide.
GPS Coordinates:
35.95746° N, 111.95547° W
Did You Know?
Members of the Navajo Nation continue to live in Canyon de Chelly!

Journal:

Date(s) Visited:

Weather conditions:

Who you were with:

Nature observations:

Special memories:

19

Havasu Falls

Due to mineral deposits of calcium carbonate and magnesium, the Havasu Falls are naturally light blue. The bright color of the water and the contrast of the deep red hues of the sandstone rock have brought visitors to the region for years. But the trip to the falls is not easy, and a round-trip 10-mile hike is needed to reach the falls. Flooding has drastically changed the appearance of the falls over the past 100 years. Havasu Falls is located in the Havasupai Reservation, and Havasu Pai translates to "people of the blue-green water." In 1975, nearly 185,000 acres of land were returned to the Havasupai Nation, which would help bring tourism into the region. When the Grand Canyon was given national park status, it protected Havasu Falls. The surrounding land around the falls was protected, meaning nothing could happen to it. This saved the falls and surrounding regions without them needing their own national park status. The falls are famous for the stunning photos taken of them and are known for the excellent swimming pool formed at the waterfall base. The water temperature stays at 70°F all year round due to the distance the Havasu Creek travels to reach the waterfall.

Best time to visit:
April to May, September to October
Pass/Permit/Fees:
3-day permit needed, between $300-$400 per person
Closest city or town:
Peach Springs, Arizona
How to get there:
Either hiking 10 miles or renting a mule to take you to the falls is an option.
GPS Coordinates:
36.2552° N, 112.6979° W
Did You Know?
The Havasu Creek passes through the Supai Village, one of the most isolated places in the United States. Helicopters deliver their food and supplies!

Journal:

Date(s) Visited:

Weather conditions:

Who you were with:

Nature observations:

Special memories:

Lake Mead National Recreation Area

Located on the border of Arizona and Nevada, the Lake Mead area is the first national recreation area in the United States. After the construction of the Hoover Dam began in 1931, a reservoir was created due to the damming of the Colorado River. This reservoir would become Lake Mead, named after the Bureau of Reclamation at the time. With recent droughts, the lake's water levels have been lowered, and the white layer of rock that encompasses the lake details how high the water levels used to be. The lake and the region around it encompass over 1.5 million acres of land, including mountains, canyons, and two lakes. Lake Mead Recreation Area is located within three of the four desert ecosystems in the entire United States: the Mojave, the Great Basin, and the Sonoran Desert. Lake Mead is nestled between two mountain ranges, the River and Muddy Mountains, which allow for hiking and climbing activities. With the vast amount of land, there are multiple ways to enjoy the region with boating, hiking, camping, and fishing. Boaters can find cliffs and beaches on the shores surrounding the lake – ideal to find a peaceful location for a day trip.

Best time to visit:
May to September
Pass/Permit/Fees:
$20 fee, good for seven consecutive days
Closest city or town:
Las Vegas, Nevada
How to get there:
Fly into Las Vegas and drive to the recreation area!
GPS Coordinates:
36.1435° N, 114.4144° W
Did You Know?
There are at least two crashed planes at the bottom of Lake Mead!

Journal:

Date(s) Visited:

Weather
conditions:

Who you were with:

Nature observations:

Special memories:

Petrified Forest National Park

The Petrified Forest is located on 346 square miles of land covering desert and badlands landscapes, known for the number of petrified trees, with many dating back 225 million years ago. The area used to be covered in trees and other plants until volcanic lava destroyed the region. The ash and lava preserved many trees, and years of erosion have revealed the trees. Many of the trees would be petrified in quartz rock, and these rocks are still in the forest and are able to be seen on the Crystal Forest Trail. Humans have been living in the region for over 8,000 years, and many artifacts have been found, including Puerco Pueblo, a village that is nearly 800 years old. Other plants, reptiles, and even dinosaur fossils have been found and studied here. Some of the most popular areas to visit in the Petrified Forest are Giants Log Trail, Jasper Forest, and Crystal Forest Trail. There are multiple designated trails that guests can walk along to explore the different regions within the park. The park has two main sections. The southern area is known for the petrified trees, while the northern part is the Painted Desert – this area has more focus on archeology and those that lived in the region.

Best time to visit:
March to May, October
Pass/Permit/Fees:
$15 bike, $20 motorcycle, $25 vehicle
Closest city or town:
Holbrook, Arizona
How to get there:
Fly into Phoenix, Flagstaff, or Albuquerque and drive along Rt. 40 to the park.
GPS Coordinates:
35.0037° N, 109.7889° W
Did You Know?
President Theodore Roosevelt made the forest a National Monument in 1906.

Journal:

Date(s) Visited:

Weather
conditions:

Who you were with:

Nature observations:

Special memories:

Saguaro National Park

Those looking for typical desert scenery and some of the largest cacti in the United States should visit Saguaro National Park. Named after the saguaro cactus that grows in the region, this park has many roads that navigate throughout the park, showcasing the cacti. Some of the oldest rocks in the park were formed nearly 1.7 billion years ago, including 1.4 billion-year-old granites, with human activity in villages created between 200 and 1450 AD. In 1961, President John F. Kennedy added an additional 16,000 acres of land to be protected, including the Saguaro National Park. There are two sections to the park that cover nearly 92,000 acres of land. The eastern side, Rincon Mountain District, has a smaller number of cacti, but you can see the mountains.
In contrast, Tucson Mountain District has a much higher number of cacti on the western side and tends to be busier. There are 165 miles of trails for hiking and paved roads for a safer walking option. Both districts of the park also allow for bicycling and horseback riding throughout the park. The park is home to nearly 1.8 million saguaro cacti, which can grow up to 60 feet and weigh about 4,800 pounds. There are 30 different species of animals in the park, including cougars, javelina, and an endangered lesser long-nosed bat!

Best time to visit:
October to April
Pass/Permit/Fees:
$14 for vehicles, $7 for bikes or motorcycles – the fee is good for seven consecutive days
Closest city or town:
Tucson, Arizona
How to get there:
Fly into Tucson, and take a quick drive to either side of the park from the city.
GPS Coordinates:
32.2967° N, 111.1666° W
Did You Know?
Saguaro cactus can live up to 200 years in the correct conditions!

Journal:

Date(s) Visited:

Weather conditions:

Who you were with:

Nature observations:

Special memories:

27

Antelope Canyon

This slot canyon is known for the iconic images of light beams shining through with unparalleled sandstone formations. The canyon was formed by erosion due to flash flooding and heavy rainy seasons that wore away the sandstone over millions of years. This resulted in deep corridors with smoothed edges. The inside of the canyon has many organic and flowing-like shapes, with the walls of the canyon measuring 120 feet tall. Antelope Canyon is divided into two sections: the upper and lower canyons. The upper canyon is known for the beams of light shining, while the lower canyon has less impressive light beams and requires climbing on ladders – but tends to be less busy! The canyon is under protection by the Navajo Nation, with the canyon under the LeChee Chapter of the nation. Only guided tours via the Navajo Nation are allowed to protect the canyons and also protect the guest from flash flooding. The Navajo know the Upper Antelope Canyon as "the place where water runs through rocks" and the lower canyon as "spiral rock arches." The name "antelope" comes from a Navajo story about antelopes that grazed in the canyon during the winter months. The Pronghorn Antelopes can still be found grazing in the region.

Best time to visit:
March to October
Pass/Permit/Fees:
$80
Closest city or town:
Page, Arizona
How to get there:
Phoenix and Las Vegas are the nearest major airports. Rent a car and drive for around five hours to reach Page, Arizona.
GPS Coordinates:
36.8619° N, 111.3743° W
Did You Know?
In 2014, the photograph *Phantom* by Peter Lik, taken in Upper Antelope Canyon, sold for a world-record amount of 6.5 million dollars.

Journal:

Date(s) Visited:

Weather conditions:

Who you were with:

Nature observations:

Special memories:

Tumacacori National Historical Park

The Tumacacori National Park covers 360 acres of protected land, including three Spanish missions. Mission San José de Tumacácori is one of Arizona's oldest mission locations. The first church was established in 1691, the second mission built was in 1750, and the third in 1756. The second mission, Calabaza, was created to mimic the San Xavier del Bac mission located near Tucson, but the building was never fully completed. The remains of the mission showcase adobe bricks and decorations built into the walls by crushing bricks. Visitors can enter the missions and view the craftsmanship of the time. The Spanish missionaries left the area, leaving the three remaining missions of Tumacácori, Calabaza, and Guevavi abandoned until 1908. The ruins of the missions were protected with historical park status in 1908 to protect and preserve the Spanish settlers' history. Besides church remains, the park is full of wildlife, plants, and trees to explore. The region sits atop the Santa Cruz River Valley, which provides the region with lush vegetation. There are hiking trails within the Tumacacori Park, such as the Anza Trail, connecting the Tubac Presidio State Site with Tumacacori. There are also options for horseback rides along the Anza Trail.

Best time to visit:
April to October
Pass/Permit/Fees:
$7, the fee is good for seven consecutive days
Closest city or town:
Nogales, Arizona
How to get there:
45 miles outside of Tucson, Arizona. It is best to fly into Tucson and rent a car to drive the distance.
GPS Coordinates:
31.5678° N, 111.0510° W
Did You Know?
You can hike four miles of the Anza Trail that runs through the park. Proof of the hike will earn you a button at the shop!

Journal:

Date(s) Visited:

Weather conditions:

Who you were with:

Nature observations:

Special memories:

Beaver Falls Trail

Located on the Supai Reservation, Beaver Falls is located on the same trail to Havasupai and Mooney Falls. This waterfall is not one fall but rather a series of smaller falls and pools created by sandstone and limestone. Similar to Havasupai Falls, calcium carbonate and magnesium cause the light color of the pool. The Havasu Creek runs through the falls and is a run-off of the Colorado River. A small dam was created on Havasu Creek to protect the falls and the pools, especially with the possibility of flooding during a heavy rainy season. Before 1910, these waterfalls at Beaver Falls were much taller, nearly 50 feet in some areas, until flooding destroyed many of the limestone ledges. These falls are much smaller in size but enjoyable for those looking for a different swimming option than the main falls. There is no current in the water, making it an excellent opportunity for swimming, and you can use tubes to float when you've arrived at the falls. This fall is a farther hike than Havasupai, and fewer people visit, making it an ideal location for a quieter escape. To see the falls requires an eight-mile round-trip hike from the designated trailhead at the campgrounds!

Best time to visit:
April to June, September to October
Pass/Permit/Fees:
3-day permit needed, between $300-$400 per person
Closest city or town:
Peach Springs, Arizona
How to get there:
Hike the 8-10 miles to reach the falls, or you have the option of renting a mule from a tour group.
GPS Coordinates:
36° 9' 44" N, 112° 42' 34" W
Did You Know?
The falls are located in the Havasupai Reservation, and Havasu Pai translates to "people of the blue-green water."

Journal:

Date(s) Visited:

Weather conditions:

Who you were with:

Nature observations:

Special memories:

Horseshoe Bend

One of the most famous photographed locations on the Colorado River, the edge overlook is 1,000 feet above the river below. It's where the name "Horseshoe Bend" comes from. The river below turns around the edge and looks like a horseshoe with a 270-degree bend. The bend is only five miles downstream from Glen Canyon Dam and Lake Powell. The bend was formed due to the Navajo sandstone, a dense type of sandstone. This acted as a natural barrier, forcing the river to make the sharp turn and thus creating Horseshoe Bend. The rock formations around the bend are made up of multiple minerals, including hematite, platinum, and garnet. The hike to the overlook is under one mile, making it ideal for those looking for less intense hikes. There are even options of taking a boat tour around the bend, offering a different perspective. The Colorado River's blue-green color is due to the extremely low water temperature – averaging 40°F! This is because the water flows from the bottom of the Glen Canyon Dam, only five miles away. Horseshoe Bend is under the Glen Canyon National Recreation Area's watch and managed by the National Park Service. These organizations have been working to make this new "it" spot safe and a great experience!

Best time to visit:
March to October
Pass/Permit/Fees:
$10 per car, $5 per motorcycle
Closest city or town:
Page, Arizona
How to get there:
Fly into Flagstaff or Phoenix and drive north on Highway 89.
GPS Coordinates:
36.8791 N, 111.5104 W
Did You Know?
The Colorado River is bound to eventually cut through the sandstone and create a natural bridge over time, but this would ruin the iconic horseshoe shape!

Journal:

Date(s) Visited:

Weather
conditions:

Who you were with:

Nature observations:

Special memories:

Lake Powell

The lake was created in 1963 after the Glen Canyon Dam's construction left the area covered in hundreds of feet of water; thus, Lake Powell was born. The dam was created to utilize the Colorado River's power and supply nearby states with water and electricity. Lake Powell is the second-largest human-made lake in the United States! It took the lake 17 years to reach the depth that it is currently at, given the lake holds 27,000,000 feet of water. The area of Lake Powell was formed by sandstone erosion over 5 million years ago. The lake was named after John Wesley Powell, a veteran of the American Civil War, and he explored the region in 1869. This lake is known for water activities, camping on the shore, and many unique rock shapes. The lake is also well known for fishing, with many different varieties of fish to catch. The land around the lake is known for many hiking trails to further explore the sandstone rocks that are famous in the region, including the famous Rainbow Bridge located near Lake Powell, one of the largest natural bridges in the world. Due to the steep cliff sides surrounding the lake, entrances are limited, with only five main entrances: two in Arizona and three in Utah.

Best time to visit:
May to August
Pass/Permit/Fees:
$30, the fee is good for seven consecutive days
Closest city or town:
Page, Arizona
How to get there:
Fly into Phoenix or Las Vegas, which requires driving four hours (from Phoenix) or eight hours (from Las Vegas) to Lake Powell.
GPS Coordinates:
37.0683° N, 111.2433° W
Did You Know?
The lake has nearly 2,000 miles of shoreline, which is almost the same as the entire west coast of the United States!

Journal:

Date(s) Visited:

Weather conditions:

Who you were with:

Nature observations:

Special memories:

Meteor Crater National Landmark

Nearly 50,000 years ago, a meteorite hit the Earth, resulting in a crater with a diameter of 0.737 miles and a depth of 560 feet. When the meteor hit the Earth, the force was equivalent to 2.5 million tons of explosives. This meteor crater is one of the most well-persevered meteors on Earth, and this is due to the young age of the crater and the dry climate further preserving it. The crater was hardly explored until 1891, when Grove Gilbert, the head of the United States Geological Survey, started to study the region, thus bringing popularity and tourism into the area. No one had successfully identified a meteor crater before, and many were suspicious about this site. In order to further preserve the inside of the crater, no solo hiking within is allowed. In order to be allowed inside the crater and to visit the floor, a guided tour is necessary. The crater was given many names since its discovery, including "Coon Mountain," "Coon Butte," and "Crater Mountain." In 1967, after attempts to make the crater public, it was given National Natural Landmark designation. The land is not under government protection due to its private ownership.

Best time to visit:
March to November
Pass/Permit/Fees:
$11 (ages 6 to 12), $20 (ages 13-59), $18 (ages 60+)
Closest city or town:
Flagstaff, Arizona
How to get there:
Fly into Flagstaff or Phoenix, Arizona. Rent a car and drive to the landmark!
GPS Coordinates:
35° 1' 41" N, 111° 1' 20" W
Did You Know?
The crater is privately owned by the Baringer family!

Journal:

Date(s) Visited:

Weather conditions:

Who you were with:

Nature observations:

Special memories:

Apache - Sitgreaves National Forest

Located in eastern Arizona, the Apache and Sitgreaves National Forest covers over two million acres of land. The Sitgreaves Forest was named after Captain Sitgreaves, who conducted scientific expeditions in the area in the 1850s, while the Apache Forest was named for the Native American tribes that lived in the region. With over 400 different species of wildlife in the area, the forest has four wilderness areas within the park to protect and educate visitors about the woods' nature, including the newly re-introduced Mexican gray wolf! The forest is known for the vast hiking trails, with over 1,000 miles of trails throughout both forests. These trails are used for hiking, horseback riding, or biking. The two woods have a total of 34 lakes and reservoirs, with over 680 miles of rivers and streams. With the many waterways and streams, these forests are considered one of the top locations for fishing in the country. Both forests have a deep history of human habitation. Throughout the woods, there are remains of pueblos (villages), showcasing carved and painted images on the pueblo walls, dating over 600-900 years old. Some of the oldest wall paintings can be seen at the Blue Crossing Campground.

Best time to visit:
March to May, October to November
Pass/Permit/Fees:
Free
Closest city or town:
Overgaard, Arizona
How to get there:
Flying into Tucson, Phoenix or Albuquerque, New Mexico are the best options, then renting a car to drive to the forest.
GPS Coordinates:
34.3885° N, 110.6170° W
Did You Know?
One chipmunk in the Apache -Sitgreaves forest can gather 165 acorns in one day!

Journal:

Date(s) Visited:

Weather
conditions:

Who you were with:

Nature observations:

Special memories:

The Wave

Some of the most famous sandstone rock formations in the Southwest are at The Wave. Located within the Coyotes Buttes North area, this region has many unparalleled rock sites, including The Second Wave, Top Rock Arch, and Sand Cove. In order to reach The Wave, a three-mile hike one way is required. There are no trails besides spaced-out markers. Visitors have to use a map or GPS to reach The Wave; this can be challenging for beginner navigators. The Wave is known for the unique rock formations of long rocks that are similar to ocean waves! Two major troughs formed 190 million years ago; the first is 62 feet wide by 188 feet long, the second trough is only 7 feet wide by 52 feet long. The lines within the troughs were formed by water flowing at different rates, and the tiny ridges were formed by alternating wind erosion. The blowing winds during the Jurassic period created deep colored hues as manganese and iron were deposited. The Wave is located within the Colorado Plateau, which is famous for the natural wonders created, including the Grand Canyon, The Arches, and Antelope Canyons. The Wave became famous after a feature in a German travel brochure in 1996!

Best time to visit:
December to February – more likely to get a permit
Pass/Permit/Fees:
Daily permit required, $9 per group
Closest city or town:
Fredonia, Arizona
How to get there:
Fly into a major airport like Las Vegas, Phoenix, or Salt Lake City, and drive to The Wave!
GPS Coordinates:
37.0424° N, 112.5122° W
Did You Know?
Only 20 people per day are allowed to hike to The Wave!

Journal:

Date(s) Visited:

Weather conditions:

Who you were with:

Nature observations:

Special memories:

White Pocket

Visitors to White Pocket can find vast swirling colorful rock formations, including domes and ridges that stand out in this one square mile region of White Pocket. This unique remote location can be found within Vermilion Cliffs National Mountain. Located east of the Coyote Bluffs South, this area is only accessible by ATV or 4-wheel-drive vehicles because of the rugged terrain and deep sand dunes. The red and orange lateral lines rise over the bluffs and the near-white "cauliflower" rock formations that have formed. The white rock formations have left geologists without an answer. Many have agreed that an earthquake triggered a sand slide that resulted in debris landing in the water and turning it into the near bleached white shade. Others believe that sandstone was left after an earthquake, then the region was underwater, and the pressure and heat over 100 million years resulted in these bizarre formations. White Pocket has many unique rock formations, including a rock that looks similar to an egg! Besides the rare rock formations, there are many native animals in the region to view, such as California Condors. While hiking to White Pocket is not encouraged, driving an off-road vehicle is the safest option. Upon arrival at White Pocket, visitors can explore the extraordinary sites.

Best time to visit:
March to May, September to October
Pass/Permit/Fees:
No permit
Closest city or town:
Jacob Lake, Arizona
How to get there:
To reach White Pocket, visitors have to travel 16 miles into Vermilion Cliffs National Park at House Rock Valley Road!
GPS Coordinates:
36.9561° N, 111.9043° W
Did You Know?
In April and May, there are wildflowers blooming, including different varieties of cactus!

Journal:

Date(s) Visited:

Weather
conditions:

Who you were with:

Nature observations:

Special memories:

Havasupai

The Havasupai Reservation is home to the Supai Village and three famous waterfalls: Havasu, Mooney, and Beaver Falls. A fourth waterfall existed until a flood in 2008 destroyed the Navajo Falls. Havasupai translates to Havasu, "blue-green water," and pai, "people," with the tribe living in the region for over 800 years. Located southwest of the Grand Canyon National Park, Havasupai is a popular location to hike among the hiking community. In order to protect the exceptional natural wonder, the Havasupai Reservation started a lottery program to limit those allowed to hike to the falls. The Havasu Falls is famed for the drastic colors of the red rock as the bright blue water rushes down the rock face! Beaver Falls tends to be a lesser-known fall, given it is located farther away, but this fall is ideal for those looking to swim in natural pools. The Havasu Creek runs through the falls and is a run-off of the Colorado River. A small dam was created on Havasu Creek to protect the falls and the pools, especially with the possibility of flooding during a heavy rainy season. The entire Havasupai region is full of distinctive colors and one-of-a-kind photo opportunities.

Best time to visit:
March to May, September to October
Pass/Permit/Fees:
Permits are needed to hike to any of the falls: 3-day permit needed, between $300-$400 per person
Closest city or town:
Peach Springs, Arizona
How to get there:
Either hike or rent a mule to take you to the falls or village.
GPS Coordinates:
36.2333° N, 112.7007° W
Did You Know?
The Supai Village is the only place in the United States that gets its mail by mule!

Journal:

Date(s) Visited:

Weather conditions:

Who you were with:

Nature observations:

Special memories:

Mount Charleston Summit

Reaching the summit of Mount Charleston will offer panoramic views of the surrounding region, including Las Vegas, Death Valley, and the Sierra Nevada Range. The peak of the mountain, at 11,916 feet, makes it one of the tallest mountains in the region. This mountain has become a favorite among locals in the region, a great way to escape the heat from the desert and even see some snow during the winter months. The two official trails, the South Loop Trail and the North Loop Trail, both require a 16-mile round-trip hike with over 4,000 feet needed to climb. Both routes take around 8 to 9 hours to complete, and most hikers choose to camp along the mountain. There is also a campground that can hold 200 sites, and this is an excellent option for those without much camping experience. For half the year, the top of Mount Charleston is covered in snow. People from around the Las Vegas area will take this opportunity to ski and snowboard. In the Southern Paiute dialect, the mountain is called Nuvagantu, which translates to "where snow sits." Mount Charleston is an excellent option for anyone looking to experience something different while in the Las Vegas region.

Best time to visit:
June to October – Snow-free months
Pass/Permit/Fees:
No permit for hiking
Closest city or town:
Indian Springs, Nevada
How to get there:
Fly into Las Vegas and drive around 45 minutes to reach the mountain base.
GPS Coordinates:
36°16'18"N 115°41'44"W
Did You Know?
Mount Charleston occupies a whopping 316,000 acres!

Journal:

Date(s) Visited:

Weather conditions:

Who you were with:

Nature observations:

Special memories:

Big Falls

Located on the eastern side of Mount Charleston, within the Kyle Canyon, is Big Falls. Both Big Falls and its sister falls, Mary Jane, are seasonal and only flow with water during the spring season. With heavy snowfall during the winter months and the spring's melting temperatures, run-off water will turn into two waterfalls in Kyle Canyon: the Mary Jane and Big Falls. The latter is the more popular option for hikers to visit, given that it has a much more dramatic drop of nearly 150-200 feet. The hike to Big Falls is just over three miles and will take around 2.5 to 3 hours to complete. During the summer, the hike can be intense due to heat, and in the winter, slippery ice can be dangerous. One of the perks of this waterfall is the covering, and the canyon walls provide shade during the day. This is ideal for allowing hikers a chance to rest and stay out of the heat in the region. Mount Charleston is known for its insane hiking trails that lead to the mountain's summit, and Big Falls is another trail that will offer rewarding views! Hikers can camp in designated camping locations or free camp options but must stay at least 200 feet away from any trails or streams.

Best time to visit:
March to April
Pass/Permit/Fees:
No permit for hiking
Closest city or town:
Indian Springs, Nevada
How to get there:
Fly into Las Vegas and drive around 45 minutes to reach the mountain base. Take the trailheads marked for Big Falls.
GPS Coordinates:
36.26897, -115.67836
Did You Know?
Mount Charleston is almost 20 degrees cooler than Las Vegas during the day and close to 30 degrees different at night!

Journal:

Date(s) Visited:

Weather conditions:

Who you were with:

Nature observations:

Special memories:

The Fire Wave

Located within the Valley of Fire State Park in Nevada, the area known as Fire Wave is popular due to its rare stripes. The state park has nearly 50,000 acres of preserved land and allows for ample hiking and exploration. The Fire Wave is a bowl-shaped depression that is lined with streaks of beige, red, and orange sandstone. The colors were created by oxidation of iron (red) and manganese (pink), with silica and bleaching that caused the white sandstone. The extraordinary colors are the main reason for the popularity among photographers! The Fire Valley and the Fire Wave formed over 150 million years ago. During this time, dinosaurs roamed the Earth! The trail to reach the Fire Wave is 1.5 miles round trip with a 175 feet elevation change; this trail is easy for most hikers. The trail to reach Fire Wave has spectacular views of the Valley of Fire, with tall sandstone bluffs rising out of the desert floor! The park is a favorite among photographers due to the rock formations, unparalleled colors, and organic movement. Some of the most popular times of the day to visit Fire Wave are at sunset and sunrise when the sky's colors reflect and add to the colors of the rocks. There are wall art and carvings from the first inhabitants, the Puebloans, in the Fire Wave region.

Best time to visit:
October to April
Pass/Permit/Fees:
$10 ($8 for Nevada residents)
Closest city or town:
Overton, Nevada
How to get there:
Fly into Las Vegas and rent a car to drive to the park.
GPS Coordinates:
36°28'47" N 114°31'36" W
Did You Know?
This is the first park established by the State of Nevada in 1935!

Journal:

Date(s) Visited:

Weather
conditions:

Who you were with:

Nature observations:

Special memories:

Calico Tanks

Calico Tanks is one of the most popular locations in the Red Rock Canyon National Conservation Area. The area encompasses 197.349 acres of land, and the sandstone walls, the Keystone Thrust, are some of the most popular regions in the area. The sandstone rocks are bright, vibrant colors of red and yellow, with grey-blue mountains in the background. The trail is 2.5 miles round trip with a 420 feet elevation gain, with a few sections of a steep incline. On the path to Calico Tanks, visitors will pass the Excelsior Stone Quarry – one of the first industries in Las Vegas. There are still sandstone cuts for visitors to view. There are multiple pools or tanks of water along the trail. At the end of the course, there is a large pool. Calico Tanks is named after the natural tank water pools at the top of the hike. The name "calico" was given to the region because of the multiple colors formatted into the rock. During the summer, these pools can be dried up, and the depth can change due to the rain and snowfall during the winter months. The top of the Calico Tanks offers a view of the Las Vegas Strip, a great place for unique photos. The region has many native plant species, including the famed Joshua tree. There is even a protected habitat for the desert tortoise!

Best time to visit:
March to May, October to November
Pass/Permit/Fees:
$15 per vehicle
Closest city or town:
Las Vegas, Nevada
How to get there:
Fly into Las Vegas and rent a car to drive to Red Rock Canyon.
GPS Coordinates:
36° 9' 51.9084" N and 115° 26' 40.4592" W
Did You Know?
Agave plants are native to this area and can be found growing throughout the park!

Journal:

Date(s) Visited:

Weather
conditions:

Who you were with:

Nature observations:

Special memories:

Griffith Peak

Located in the Spring Mountains, only 28 miles northwest of Las Vegas, this peak is a favorite among hikers. Griffith Peak is 11,056 feet tall, making it the third-highest peak in the Spring Mountain Range. Reaching the top of the peak offers the eastern view of Las Vegas, with views of Red Rock Canyon and the Calico Basins, which are not visible from other mountains in the region. Griffith Peak also offers one of the best views of Mt. Charleston in the entire area. There are two primary trails: the South Loop and the Harris Springs Trail. The hike to the South Loop peak is 9.4 miles and is quite difficult for beginner hikers, but the trail has a lot of tree shade, making it more comfortable for hikers. Throughout the trail, deep lush forest areas offer different scenery than the desert region of Southern Nevada. During the winter months, the peak is covered in ice and snow, making hiking more difficult to navigate unless with the correct equipment. Camping along Griffith Peak is popular, although fires are not permitted! The region has been affected by wildfires, and the damage can be seen throughout the mountain with charred trees. Deer and native birds can be seen throughout the trails, especially in the morning. Looking around the rock formation on the mountain, fossils can be found in the stone!

Best time to visit:
May to October
Pass/Permit/Fees:
$8 per car
Closest city or town:
Mt. Charleston
How to get there:
Fly into Las Vegas and rent a car to drive to Griffith Peak.
GPS Coordinates:
36.2322° N, 115.6461° W
Did You Know?
On a clear day, over 150 miles are visible from the peak!

Journal:

Date(s) Visited:

Weather
conditions:

Who you were with:

Nature observations:

Special memories:

Cathedral Rock

This is one of the most popular trails around Sedona, Arizona, only measuring one mile, yet it can be difficult with an elevation gain of 608 feet. The hike is closer to a rock scramble to reach the top! The trail will take hikers in between the towering buttes with the red striped sandstone. Looking at the Cathedral Rock, four main rock formations can be seen. These sandstone buttes are located within the Coconino National Forest. Cathedral Rock was formed by the erosion from water and wind over millions of years. Cathedral Rock was formed by the Permian Schnebly Hill formation, while the red sandstone was created by sand dunes from a prehistoric shoreline. Oak Creek runs alongside Cathedral Rock, and this area is often called "Red Rock Crossing" by the Navajo and Hopi Native Americans. This region is considered to be sacred, with references to this being the home of gods and the birthplace of men and women, according to the local Native Americans. Reaching the top of Cathedral Rock will offer views of the landscape in Coconino National Forest. One of the reasons for the popularity is the vortex that many believe is present here. Many claims that the vortices release feminine energy and leave visitors feeling more creative and even rested.

Best time to visit:
March to May, October to November
Pass/Permit/Fees:
$5 per car
Closest city or town:
Sedona, Arizona
How to get there:
Fly into Flagstaff or Phoenix airport and rent a car to drive to Sedona. There are also shuttles that transport from Phoenix to Sedona.
GPS Coordinates:
34.8200° N, 111.7932° W
Did You Know?
Cathedral Rock was given that name because it represents a grand cathedral!

Journal:

Date(s) Visited:

Weather conditions:

Who you were with:

Nature observations:

Special memories:

Liberty Bell Arch

Located in the famed Lake Mead National Recreational Area, Liberty Bell Arch is named after the Liberty Bell in Philadelphia. Formed over time through wind and water erosion, a hole shaped like a bell was included in the rocks. The trail to Liberty Bell is six miles round trip with an 800 feet elevation gain. The hike is considered to be strenuous and is closed during the summer months due to the insane heat and danger of it. Similar geological formations can be found at the famed Arches National Monument. For those looking to see this type of formation but not wanting to make the strenuous hike, Arches is a great option. The hike to Liberty Bell Arch offers a glimpse of the past history of the area, including cable-car ore from when the region was used for magnesium mining. The old mine's entrance is still visible, and some hikers will enter and look. Luckily, the mine is not deep and shows the last drill holes on the back. Reaching the top of the trail will also offer views of Black Canyon Overlook and 1,000 feet above the Colorado River flowing through. Located near the Liberty Bell Arch Trail, another track leads to the natural hot springs – many people will come here to relax during their hike.

Best time to visit:
October to March – the trail is not open during the summer months
Pass/Permit/Fees:
$25 per vehicle
Closest city or town:
Boulder City, Nevada
How to get there:
Fly into Las Vegas, as it is the closest major airport. Rent a car and drive to the trailhead.
GPS Coordinates:
35.9749° N, 114.7242° W
Did You Know?
North of the arch is the famed Hoover Dam.

Journal:

Date(s) Visited:

Weather
conditions:

Who you were with:

Nature observations:

Special memories:

Watson Lake

Surrounded by granite boulders, Watson Lake is an ideal getaway from Arizona's summer heat – even if swimming is banned. Watson Lake is one of two reservoirs in the Granite Dells. Both reservoirs were formed in the 1900s after the Chino Valley built a dam on Granite Creek. This resulted in the creation of the lakes. In 1997, the City of Prescott purchased the land around the lake to be used as recreational land for visitors. After the purchase, the lake is now located on 380 acres of land. The hiking trails that surround the lake are known for spring flower blooms. Some of the visitors' favorite activities to do are hiking, fishing, boating, kayaking, and camping along the shores. Fishing is very popular in this region, with rainbow trout, largemouth bass, and bluegill fish! In 2019, a fish ladder was created to help breed and re-habituate fish in the lake. Besides fish, the region is home to many birds such as Golden Eagles and Canyon Wrens. The Granite Dells located near the lake is one of the most popular attractions in the region. Within the lake, there are granite boulders; decreased water levels over the years have left white rings around the lake.

Best time to visit:
April to October
Pass/Permit/Fees:
$3
Closest city or town:
Prescott, Arizona
How to get there:
Fly into Phoenix, Arizona, and rent a car to drive to the lake.
GPS Coordinates:
34.5875° N, 112.4180° W
Did You Know?
Mercury mining caused Watson Lake to be polluted, and thus no swimming is allowed.

Journal:

Date(s) Visited:

Weather
conditions:

Who you were with:

Nature observations:

Special memories:

Canyon de Chelly

Canyon de Chelly covers 83,840 acres of land and houses three major canyons: de Chelly, del Muerto, and Monument. The canyons were formed by thousands of years of streams that cut through the region. Some of the most popular geological features are Spider Rock, Mummy Cave, and Antelope House Overlook. Prior to being a national monument, the region was home to the Navajo people; the entire Canyon de Chelly region is currently owned by the Navajo Tribal Trust! This is the only national park that is owned and managed by another trust – the Navajo's. The park still has evidence of the original people in the region, with the White and Antelope House Ruins. Many of the ruins sit 600 feet off the cliffs and have over 70 rooms. These historical locations within the region showcase carved and drawn images within walls. These images have been studied to help understand the depiction of life and those living during those times. The canyon has two main roads – the South Rim and the North Rim. Both roads allow for scenic overlooks of Canyon de Chelly. A seasonal stream will form after snow and rain during the winter – the Chinle Wash will form at the lower end of the canyon floor.

Best time to visit:
April to May, September to October
Pass/Permit/Fees:
No entrance fees
Closest city or town:
Chinle, Arizona
How to get there:
Taking either North Rim or South Rim Drive will allow views of the park from the car. To visit the canyon, visitors must travel with a park ranger or Navajo guide.
GPS Coordinates:
36.1336° N, 109.4694° W
Did You Know?
Members of the Navajo Nation continue to live in Canyon de Chelly!

Journal:

Date(s) Visited:

Weather conditions:

Who you were with:

Nature observations:

Special memories:

Tonto Natural Bridge

This unique natural wonder is known for its one-of-a-kind bridges and the largest travertine bridge in the world. A travertine bridge is created when water travels beneath limestone and calcium carbonate to form a natural travertine bridge. Millions of years of volcanic lava, seawater, and erosion formed a travertine dam. A lodge was created by the man who discovered the bridge, David Gowan, and the lodge is also home to their heirlooms. The bridge is 183 feet high and with tunnels over 400 feet long; the widest point is 150 feet. Located in the Tonto National Forest, this park is great for hiking! At the opening of the bridge, there is a natural waterfall following the winter season after rain. With three hiking trails that all lead to the bridge, each track showcases the park's different wonders. Most courses will take two hours to reach. For those not wanting to hike, the bridge is visible from the car parking lot. Hikers are able to explore underneath the natural bridge! This Tonto Natural Forest State Park is one of the smallest parks in the state, at only 161 acres in total. The region near the bridge is lusher than other locations in the state due to the high elevation, allowing for more snow melting.

Best time to visit:
March to May, September to October
Pass/Permit/Fees:
$7 per adult
Closest city or town:
Payson, Arizona
How to get there:
Fly into Phoenix, Arizona, and rent a car to drive to the bridge.
GPS Coordinates:
34.3229° N, 111.4544° W
Did You Know?
The bridge was discovered in 1877 by a Scottish man, David Gowan.

Journal:

Date(s) Visited:

Weather conditions:

Who you were with:

Nature observations:

Special memories:

Labyrinth Slot Canyon

This slotted canyon is very underrated. Located on the Green River, it's only reachable by kayak or paddleboard. It is one of the most popular slot canyons in the Antelope Canyon, also located in Arizona. At some of the canyon's tallest parts, walls reach up to 30 feet tall, with the canyon's length stretching almost one mile deep. The smooth sandstone walls are prime examples of natural erosion and the force of rivers on sandstone. The entrance to the canyon is nearly 11 miles from the closest marina on Lake Powell. The canyon was accessible by foot before the creation of Lake Powell in 1972. This slotted canyon is an excellent alternative to Antelope Canyon – where lines can be very long, and you have to pay to visit, unlike Labyrinth Canyon. You can kayak or paddleboard through some sections until the walls get too thin or the water runs dry. Slotted canyons are formed after millions of years of water rushing past either sand or limestone; slotted canyons are rare formations. For those nervous about navigating to and from the canyon alone, there are many tours that visitors can take! Labyrinth Slot Canyon tends to be forgotten because it's not as famous as Antelope Canyon, but this canyon is as beautiful as Antelope!

Best time to visit:
May to September
Pass/Permit/Fees:
Only marine fees to park
Closest city or town:
Page, Arizona
How to get there:
Fly into Phoenix or Las Vegas, which requires driving four hours (from Phoenix) or eight hours (from Las Vegas) to Lake Powell.
GPS Coordinates:
34.5849.18° N, 101.557.6° W
Did You Know?
Many of the slotted canyons in North America are located in Arizona!

Journal:

Date(s) Visited:

Weather
conditions:

Who you were with:

Nature observations:

Special memories:

Cibecue Falls

The Cibecue Falls are one of the most hidden and secluded waterfalls in Arizona. The Cibecue Falls are located on the Tonto National Forest's eastern edge and within the Fort Apache Reservation. The trail to reach the falls is 3.5 to 4 miles, taking around three to four hours, and can be problematic in some course sections. The trail can be on the more difficult side, with a 400-foot elevation gain, significant steps on boulders, and crossing streams that can be hard to navigate. The Cibecue Falls path follows the creek and has small swimming pools and waterfalls from large rocks in the water. The waterfall drops across the sandstone with high red sandstone canyon walls surrounding the pool on both sides. The waterfall is located within the Cibecue Canyon, with the Cibecue Creek feeding the falls. During dry seasons the waterfall can dry up; it's best to visit following a rainy season when the waterfall is the fullest. The 80-foot falls are full of mineral blue water that allows for cooling off after the hike. Besides viewing the falls, some trails follow along Cibecue Creek. When visiting Cibecue Falls, make sure to be aware of the weather, given that flash flooding is a danger in these areas.

Best time to visit:
April to October
Pass/Permit/Fees:
$30 permit
Closest city or town:
Cibecue, Arizona
How to get there:
Fly into Phoenix and rent a car to drive to Tonto National Forest.
GPS Coordinates:
33.8550° N, 110.5475° W
Did You Know?
There is another waterfall nearby: the Apache Falls!

Journal:

Date(s) Visited:

Weather
conditions:

Who you were with:

Nature observations:

Special memories:

Sycamore Falls

This extraordinary waterfall is located only 1.5 hours south of the Grand Canyon. Situated within the Kaibab National Forest, the area covers 1.6 million acres of land, with many sites evidence of previous volcanic lava. The falls received their name from the vast amount of Sycamore trees in the park. The photos from the region offer an insight into the beauty of the area. The Willow Falls run into a natural stone pool, dropping 70 feet, with dramatic basalt cliffs towering above the falls. The canyon is the second largest canyon in the red rock country of Arizona and a popular location among locals. The main trail, Sycamore Rim Trail, is an 11-mile total loop. Throughout the path, there are many lookout points. With five entry points on the trail, you can access the falls with only a one- or two-mile walk – or walk the entire loop. The waterfall is seasonal, and during a drought or deep in the winter, there won't be Falls. During the winter, the region will be covered in snow! While during the summer, the basaltic walls are popular for rock climbing and slacklining. The spring is one of the best times to visit the falls. Following the winter, melting snow will create the strongest water flow of the year.

Best time to visit:
March to October
Pass/Permit/Fees:
None
Closest city or town:
Williams, Arizona
How to get there:
Fly into Flagstaff or Phoenix and rent a car to drive to Sycamore Falls trailhead.
GPS Coordinates:
35.137947 N, -112.027880 W
Did You Know?
The sunsets behind the falls and is one of the best times to take photos.

Journal:

Date(s) Visited:

Weather
conditions:

Who you were with:

Nature observations:

Special memories:

Salome Jug

Salome Canyon, or the Salome Jug, is located within the Sierra Ancha Mountains. The Salome Wilderness Area encompasses 18,530 acres within the Tonto National Forest. The region has been home to prehistoric Salado Indians with evidence of the previous residents around the park. The canyon has two sections, the Upper Salome Canyon and the lower canyon known as "The Jug." These canyons are known for being a natural water park, with swimming and water rafting. The Salome Creek runs through granite walls. The trail follows the creek and offers many opportunities to swim! One of the most famous trail regions is the end of a 30-foot cliff that many brave hikers use to jump into the water. Farther hiking onto the trail will show natural water slides that were created by years of erosion. Hikers will slide down the rocks and enter into pools of water – the erosion creates a smooth surface! The towering granite walls show the signs of erosion and have been smoothed over the years. The best time to visit Salome Jug is during the spring season when the water run-off is the strongest – although the water will be the coldest. This a popular place to visit during the summer season and a great way to escape the intense Arizona summer heat.

Best time to visit:
May to September
Pass/Permit/Fees:
None
Closest city or town:
Young, Arizona
How to get there:
Located outside of Phoenix – fly into the city and rent a car to drive to Salome Jug.
GPS Coordinates:
33.7712° N, 111.1357° W
Did You Know?
The trail to Salome Jug used to be a jeep run, a favorite among off-road vehicles!

Journal:

Date(s) Visited:

Weather conditions:

Who you were with:

Nature observations:

Special memories:

Walnut Canyon

Walnut Canyon is known for the extraordinary rock formations and the ancient pueblos nestled in the rock. The canyon sits on the Colorado Plateau and cuts through the Permian Kaibab Limestone, which gives it its crossbedding. The canyon is known for the limestone cliffs that were created over 60 million years ago. The canyon has three main sections: the upper layer is light-colored, the middle is darker, and the bottom walls are a nearly white shade. The canyon has a diverse ecosystem with cacti in the Upper Sonoran Desert, and the cool areas have Douglas firs. Around the rim, you'll find juniper forest and ponderosa pines! The region has various wildlife, with coyotes, elks, and mountain lions living in the area, including 121 different bird species. It was created by the Sinagua, a pre-Columbian group that lived in the canyon from 1100 to 1250 AD. Sinagua is Spanish for "without water." Remnants of the group are still in the canyon, with 25 cliffside rooms still preserved. Walnut Canyon was given national monument status in 1915 by President Wilson to protect the historic cliff dwellings. There are multiple trails, with the Island Trail being one of the most popular trails, showcasing 25 cliff dwelling rooms! The rooms were created by limestone rocks held together by clay walls.

Best time to visit:
March to October
Pass/Permit/Fees:
$15 per person, the fee is good for seven consecutive days
Closest city or town:
Cosnino, Arizona
How to get there:
Fly into Flagstaff or Phoenix and rent a car to drive to the entrance of the canyon.
GPS Coordinates:
35.1717° N, 111.5093° W
Did You Know?
There are still black marks on the walls and ceilings on the cliff dwelling rooms from the Sinagua fires!

Journal:

Date(s) Visited:

Weather conditions:

Who you were with:

Nature observations:

Special memories:

Wupatki National Monument

The Wupatki National Monument offers insight into the life of those that lived in the region thousands of years ago. Wupatki is nestled between the Painted Desert and the ponderosa highlands, with the ancient pueblos littered in between over 35,422 acres of protected land. Some of the oldest inhabited pueblos were dated to 500 AD. The Sinagua Pueblo is located within Wupatki. This pueblo was created with 100 rooms and a community room – the most prominent building for over 50 miles. There are several main ruins and at least 800 other ruins showcasing the previous structures and pueblos that are scattered around the desert. This differs from other ruins, where there were one or two buildings close together – these were separate from each other. The Wupatki Pueblo has many plants that are different from others in the region; this is due to it being 2,000 feet below sea level. The Wupatki had a house with over 300 people when it was in use! The site was registered as a national historic place in 1966, and this protected the treasured area. Besides the ancient pueblo, there are volcanic and lava ruins from when the region was filled with volcanos. The first archeological survey of the area was conducted in 1921!

Best time to visit:
March to October
Pass/Permit/Fees:
$25 for vehicles, $20 for motorcycles
Closest city or town:
Flagstaff, Arizona
How to get there:
Fly into Flagstaff or Phoenix. Rent a car and drive to the monument.
GPS Coordinates:
35.5611° N, 111.3922° W
Did You Know?
"Wupatki" means "tall house" in the Hopi language!

Journal:

Date(s) Visited:

Weather conditions:

Who you were with:

Nature observations:

Special memories:

Camelback Mountain

The Camelback Mountain is one of the most famous mountains in the Phoenix region, with exceptional views of the city. Camelback Mountain is located in the city of Phoenix, with houses and businesses located around the entire mountain. The mountain towers 2,704 feet over the area, and the hike to the top is 1.5 miles one way and has an elevation of 1,264 feet. Although there are two main trails – the Echo Canyon Trail and the Cholla Trail, both taking around 3 hours – the elevation makes it challenging for beginner hikers. There are multiple hikes for beginner hikers—Bobby's Rock Trail circles around the base of the mountain. The Camelback Mountain has been used as a holy site for the Native Americans who live in the Salt River Valley. There's a famous location on the mountain, "Praying Monk," where the red sandstone formation looks like a man kneeling in prayer. The mountain was a reservation for the Salt River Pima and the Maricopa Native Americans spanning over a million acres. Studying the mountain concluded that the mountain comprises two separate rock formations: the bottom is Precambrian granite, made 1.5 billion years ago, and the top is made of sandstone from 25 million years ago! Visiting the mountain is best in the morning or evening. This helps to avoid the intense summer heat.

Best time to visit:
March to May, October to November
Pass/Permit/Fees:
$10 for parking
Closest city or town:
Phoenix, Arizona
How to get there:
Fly into Phoenix and drive to the mountain trailhead to make the hike up.
GPS Coordinates:
33.5151° N, 111.9619° W
Did You Know?
The record for the fastest ascent to the top was 16 minutes, set by a 19-year-old male!

Journal:

Date(s) Visited:

Weather conditions:

Who you were with:

Nature observations:

Special memories:

Mount Lemmon Scenic Byway

Known as one of Arizona's most scenic drives, the byway takes drivers up Mount Lemmon, located in the Santa Catalina Mountain Range. The mountain is surrounded by the Coronado National Forest, which has been affected by wildfires in recent years. The drive, also called Catalina Highway, or the Sky Island Scenic byway, is about 27 miles one way and climbs up over 9,000 feet in elevation. The drive takes a minimum of two hours to travel. During this drive, visitors will experience multiple types of vegetation. The mountain base has desert terrain, while the top of the mount has thick, lush forests. Throughout the drive, there are many different rock formations. There are rest areas on the drive that offer a 180-degree view of the surrounding regions below, including the famous Windy Point that provides an overlook of the Tucson valley below. The top of Mount Lemmon has a ski valley for the winter months, giving locals that live in the surrounding deserts a chance to ski or snowboard. The byway is open all year, with the spring and summer months the best time to visit. This offers a great option to escape the insane summer Tucson heat. Located near the top of Mount Lemmon is the town of Summerhaven, where supplies for many summers and winter recreational activities can be rented from.

Best time to visit:
March to September
Pass/Permit/Fees:
$5 per vehicle
Closest city or town:
Tucson, Arizona
How to get there:
Fly or drive into the Tucson region, and drive to the entrance of the scenic byway.
GPS Coordinates:
32° 26' 36.3012" N and 110° 47' 17.2392" W
Did You Know?
The temperature difference between the base and top can be over 30 degrees.

Journal:

Date(s) Visited:

Weather conditions:

Who you were with:

Nature observations:

Special memories:

Organ Pipe Cactus National Monument

Located at the very south of Arizona, only miles from the Mexican border, the Organ Pipe Cactus is an International Biosphere (UNESCO) reserve declared in 1977. In 1937, the land was donated by the state of Arizona and made a national monument. The protection of the area has allowed for plants and animals to thrive! The region covers 517 square miles of protected land and is the only place in the United States where senita and organ pipe cacti grow. Location is very important for organ pipe cacti, as the winter months can kill any new growth. Cacti with bumps of wavy pipes are prime evidence of a cold season. The cactus is originally from dry tropic environments. Following the last ice age, the cactus started to migrate north. This region of organ pipe cactus has been dated to the Sonoran Desert around 3,500 years ago. This type of cactus can live up to 150 years; it takes 35 years before they produce flowers. The cacti's flowers are only open at night towards mid-morning and in May and June months. There are two scenic drives through the monument: Ajo Mountain Drive and Puerto Blanco Drive. The Ajo drive is the most popular, and with 21 miles of road, it is also the most popular biking trail. The Puerto Blanco drive is made up of two sections, North and South, and the loop is 41 miles in total and takes around three to five hours to drive round trip.

Best time to visit:
October to May
Pass/Permit/Fees:
$12 per car
Closest city or town:
Ajo, Arizona
How to get there:
Fly into Phoenix or Tucson and drive down to the park.
GPS Coordinates:
32.0878° N, 112.9059° W
Did You Know?
These cacti get their name from the many stems (or arms) that grow off the cactus!

Journal:

Date(s) Visited:

Weather conditions:

Who you were with:

Nature observations:

Special memories:

Kartchner Caverns

Discovered by two people in 1974 that were exploring the limestone hills in the Whetstone Mountains, the pair kept this cavern a secret until 1978. The caverns are limestone and filled with speleothem, a mineral deposit that is standard in caves. These form typical stalagmites and stalactites that are found inside caves. Inside Kartchner Cavern, the speleothems have been growing for over 50,000 years. Special precautions have been taken to protect and preserve the cave and the growing speleothems within. The caverns were formed over 330 million years ago after layers of sedimentary rock and fossils were formed into limestone. Rainwater and other forms of groundwater dissolved into air pockets in the ground, forming cave rooms. Over time, the erosion of water created vast spaces! The Kartchner Cavern is considered a "living" cave because the formations within are still growing. There are two main points for tourists' viewing: the Throne Room and the Big Room. There are the "World's Largest Soda Straw" stalactites, measuring at 21 feet in the Throne Room, with a 58-foot column! In the Big Room, there is the world's most extensive formation of brushite moonmilk. This room is closed during the summer months because a colony of over 2,000 cave bats uses it as a nursery roost. During this time, the bats are born and live in the cave, eating any insects inside the cavern!

Best time to visit:
Year-round, but some of the cave is closed in the summer due to bats
Pass/Permit/Fees:
$7 per vehicle, and tours of the cave cost additional fees
Closest city or town:
Benson, Arizona
How to get there:
Fly into Tucson and drive to Kartchner Caverns.
GPS Coordinates:
31.8366° N, 110.3489° W
Did You Know?
Over 60% of the cave system is not available to the public!

Journal:

Date(s) Visited:

Weather conditions:

Who you were with:

Nature observations:

Special memories:

Hoover Dam

Located on the border of Arizona and Nevada, this arch-gravity dam is one of the most famous dams in the United States. The Hoover Dam's construction occurred between 1931 and 1936, created to help the economy during the Great Depression. The dam was constructed to harvest the Colorado River's energy, and the Lake Mead Reservoir was created as a result of the dam. Lake Mead is the largest reservoir by volume in the United States. The top of the dam towers 530 feet above Black Canyon and the Colorado River below. The generators within the dam provide power and water utilities for Nevada, Arizona, and California. When the Hoover Dam was created, it was the largest dam in the world! Engineers decided on the Black Canyon and Boulder Canyon region because they could support the dam's creation. The town of Boulder City was created to house and support the 10,000 to 20,000 workers needed to complete the project. The massive arch bridge located in front of the Hoover Dam was the first concrete-steel arch bridge built in the United States and the widest concrete arch bridge in the Western Hemisphere. The region around the Hoover Dam is full of hiking trails through the geological wonders of the area. Visitors can see the water level decline around the dam and the surrounding rocks alongside Lake Mead.

Best time to visit:
All year
Pass/Permit/Fees:
Free to visit, but tours cost additional fees
Closest city or town:
Boulder City, Nevada
How to get there:
Fly into Las Vegas, the closest major airport. Rent a car and drive to the dam!
GPS Coordinates:
36.0161° N, 114.7377° W
Did You Know?
When the dam was completed, there were 4,360,000 cubic yards of concrete used! This is enough to create a hypothetical highway from San Francisco to New York.

Journal:

Date(s) Visited:

Weather
conditions:

Who you were with:

Nature observations:

Special memories:

Chiricahua National Monument

Also called "Wonderland of Rocks," the Chiricahua National Monument will have visitors wondering if they are still on Earth. The rock spires stand among tall trees and offer a unique alternative to the typical Arizona landscape. The distinctive rock formations were given monument status in 1924 to protect the hoodoos and balance rocks. Hoodoos, or tent rocks, are tall, thin rock spires formed at the bottom of an arid drainage basin. The balancing rocks in the area are naturally occurring and are also known as precarious boulders. The region was created after an insane volcanic eruption that occurred 27 million years ago. The rock formations were previously volcanic ash that has since eroded over time and made Chiricahua's treasured formation. The park has Fort Bowie National Historic Site, the remains from the fort and cemetery created in the 1860s. The region has 17 miles of a trail system that takes hikers around the park. Some trails will take you into canyons, while others will pass by rock spires. There are more accessible hikes for beginner hikers – the Silver Spur Meadow Trail follows Bonita Creek and is only 1.2 miles! There are even strenuous hikes, like Heart of Rocks, which is a 7.3-mile round-trip hike with 1,500 feet in elevation gain. During the winter months, snow can be found throughout the region.

Best time to visit:
March to May, September to November
Pass/Permit/Fees:
None
Closest city or town:
Wilcox, Arizona
How to get there:
The area is very isolated, with the closest major airport being Tucson– renting a car is necessary to reach the rocks!
GPS Coordinates:
32.0136° N, 109.3423° W
Did You Know?
There is a cabin in the park that was home to Swedish immigrants in 1887!

Journal:

Date(s) Visited:

Weather conditions:

Who you were with:

Nature observations:

Special memories:

Coconino Lava River Cave

Coconino Lava River Cave formed over 700,000 years ago after a volcanic vent erupted near Hart Prairie. The cave was created after the outside of the lava cooled, and the inside continued to flow. The rate of cooling caused the geological phenomena of Coconino Lava River Cave to form. These include rippling lava fields, lava spiral, and decorative lava ropes. The cooling of the lava caused the surface of the cave to be smooth – this can be dangerous with icy conditions. The cave is 0.75 miles long and the longest lava cave in Arizona. Even during the summer season, the temperature of the cave is around 40 degrees, and it can even have ice inside. Even during the summer, make sure to wear long sleeves and long pants when going to the caves – it gets chilly! The cave's height can range from 2 feet to over 30 feet high. One of the lava cave's unique features is the "Y-intersections," where two large tubes combine into one tube. Free camping is allowed, but make sure to camp at least one mile away from the entrance! From the parking lot to the entrance, the trail is only 0.4 miles, a straightforward walk for visitors.

Best time to visit:
May to September
Pass/Permit/Fees:
No fee
Closest city or town:
Fort Valley, Arizona
How to get there:
Phoenix and Las Vegas are two major airports in the region. Visitors can rent a car and drive to the lava tubes.
GPS Coordinates:
35.3424° N, 111.8363° W
Did You Know?
The inside of the cave stays around 42 degrees even during the summer season!

Journal:

Date(s) Visited:

Weather
conditions:

Who you were with:

Nature observations:

Special memories:

Desert Botanical Garden

The Desert Botanical Garden is located in Phoenix, Arizona, and encompasses 55 acres of land. The gardens were created in 1937 by the Arizona Cactus and Native Flora Society. The Desert Botanical Garden now has 50,000 plants with 379 rare, endangered, or threatened status species. The garden has created a seed bank that stores frozen seeds and pollen to help regenerate the rare species. Over two-thirds of the total species of cactus are in the garden's collection.

Similarly, the garden has 186 of the 212 species of agave, making this one of the world's most prominent collections. The garden has plants from around the world thriving in the desert. Besides native plants, there are also many pieces of natural sculptures with plants being incorporated into the art. After sunset, the garden comes to life in a new way, with lanterns and lights illuminating the paths around the grounds. The park has a network of trails that are split into quarter-mile loops, leading into one main track. The tracks are themed with different topics, such as conservation, desert plants, desert wildflowers, and a section on the people of the Sonoran Desert. This is an excellent way for visitors to learn about the history of the Phoenix region.

Best time to visit:
All year
Pass/Permit/Fees:
$25 per adult
Closest city or town:
Phoenix, Arizona
How to get there:
Fly or drive into the Phoenix region and drive to the garden.
GPS Coordinates:
33.4618° N, 111.9446° W
Did You Know?
The creeping devil cactus was the first cactus planted in 1939!

Journal:

Date(s) Visited:

Weather
conditions:

Who you were with:

Nature observations:

Special memories:

Vermilion Cliffs National Monument

This unspoiled and protected wilderness encompasses 280,000 acres of land. This includes the Paria Plateau, Vermilion Cliffs, and Coyote Buttes! The elevation in the region goes from 3,100 to 6,500 feet above sea level. The Vermilion Cliffs are an escarpment formation, which is long, steep slopes primarily found at the edge of a plateau. These cliffs are made of sandstone, siltstone, limestone, and shale. The cliffs tower above the valley floor, with many famous cliffs located around the area. The entire region is full of bright-colored sandstone due to iron-rich oxide pigments with evidence of millions of years of erosion. The United States Government gave the region National Monument status in 2000 to protect the untouched territory from being ruined. The Coyote Buttes have the bright rainbowed color of the area, with tall buttes standing above the floor. There are even thousands of dinosaur tracks that are dated back 190 million years. Coyote Buttes Trail is one of the most popular and demanding hiking trails, with 24 miles that can take over 11 hours to complete. The region is also home to the Paria Canyon, a slotted canyon. Paria is Paiute for "muddy water." There are two state-created campgrounds, but free camping on the Bureau of Land Management is also a popular choice.

Best time to visit:
March to May, September to October
Pass/Permit/Fees:
$10 per vehicle, some trails require a permit
Closest city or town:
Page, Arizona
How to get there:
Fly into a major airport like Las Vegas, Phoenix, or Salt Lake City, and drive to the monument.
GPS Coordinates:
36.8625° N, 111.8270° W
Did You Know?
The region is home to the endangered California condors, but through a hatch and raising/breeding program, the condor population is growing.

Journal:

Date(s) Visited:

Weather
conditions:

Who you were with:

Nature observations:

Special memories:

Humphreys Peak

The highest natural point and the second highest peak in the state of Arizona, Humphreys Peak towers at 12,637 feet. This mountain is also a part of the highest group of dormant volcanic peaks, the San Francisco Peaks. The San Francisco Volcanic Field is made up of 600 volcanoes that all range in age from 6 million years to 1,000 years old. Humphreys Peak is the tallest in the region. The last eruption in the area was 940 years ago when the Sunset Crater exploded, blowing a hole in the mountain's side. Eruptions took place between 1 million and 400,000 years ago. Humphreys Peak is an eroded stratovolcano. *Dokoo'osliid* is the name for Humphreys Peak in Navajo. This mountain is one of the four sacred peaks in the Navajo culture; they are a part of their creation story. One of the most popular hikes to the peak, the North Kaibab Trail, is 4.8 miles one way. The trailhead starts at the Arizona Snowbowl ski resort, which is located in the Coconino National Forest. The peak is covered in snow during the winter months and a favorite for many skiers. Camping is only allowed below 11,400 feet of elevation and not near the skiing slopes! The top of the mountain can have winds gusting over 50 mph.

Best time to visit:
June to October
Pass/Permit/Fees:
$5 to hike
Closest city or town:
Flagstaff, Arizona
How to get there:
Fly into Flagstaff or Phoenix, Arizona. Rent a car and drive to the mountain!
GPS Coordinates:
35.3467° N, 111.6785° W
Did You Know?
Local legend claims that Humphreys Peak is part of the San Francisco Peaks because people believe they can see San Francisco from the top – this is not true!

Journal:

Date(s) Visited:

Weather
conditions:

Who you were with:

Nature observations:

Special memories:

Fossil Creek Falls

Fossil Creek Falls is popular among locals to help escape the summer heat! The falls are located between Coconino and Tonto National Forest, giving the region some of the best-protected lands. Fossil Creek Falls is located in the Fossil Creek Canyon, which is two miles from the falls. The canyon is 1,600 feet deep, and Fossil Creek Falls emits 20,000 gallons of water per minute, staying around 72°F year-round. The water in the creek is full of calcium carbonate. The water flows from a spring and creates travertine (limestone deposit) dams downstream. The creek's water supply supports a wide variety of plants and animals in the region, almost 200 different species. Archeologists believe that the creek was used as a watershed for the people who have been in the region for over 10,000 years. The Yavapai and Apache people that live in the area used the creek. In 2008, barriers were created to help reduce the number of invasive species that had been introduced. This was done to help maximize the number of native fish that thrive in the creek. The trail to reach Fossil Creek is 2.6 miles round trip and easy for all hiking levels. The falls have deep pools, and many use the creek for swimming, kayaking, and even snorkeling – some people even jump off the 25-foot cliff.

Best time to visit:
May to October
Pass/Permit/Fees:
$6 per vehicle
Closest city or town:
Camp Verde, Arizona
How to get there:
Fly into Flagstaff or Phoenix, Arizona. Rent a car and drive to the trailhead.
GPS Coordinates:
34.4051° N, 111.6140° W
Did You Know?
Fossil Creek is one of the two streams in all of Arizona that is included in the National Wild and Scenic Rivers System.

Journal:

Date(s) Visited:

Weather
conditions:

Who you were with:

Nature observations:

Special memories:

Apache Falls

Located in the Salt River Canyon, the Apache Falls is popular due to the easy one-mile round-trip hike, and it takes around 10 minutes. The entire Salt River Canyon region encompasses 32,101 acres of land. Apache Falls is one of the highlights in the area, and it also includes tubing, paddle boarding, and fishing! Apache Falls is part of a river that gives the falls ample water flow throughout the year, unlike other Arizona waterfalls that are part of a creek. The Salt River area is home to much wildlife – deer, fox, skunks, and even river otters visit the riverbanks during the summer. Following the winter snow and rain, the water flow is the most powerful during the spring season, although with much colder temperatures than the summer. The falls are located on the San Carlos Apache Tribe Reservation and can be reached from the White Mountain Apache Salt River Canyon Recreation Area. The falls are not very tall or impressive in comparison to other falls in the region, but the large swimming area around the falls is very popular – including for cliff jumping off the sides. The rock formations in the region offer significant steps and lounging space for visitors of the area.

Best time to visit:
May to October
Pass/Permit/Fees:
$15 per vehicle
Closest city or town:
Globe, Arizona
How to get there:
Fly into Flagstaff or Phoenix, Arizona. Rent a car and drive to Fort Apache Reservation to find the trailhead.
GPS Coordinates:
33.7982° N, 110.4968° W
Did You Know?
This is one of the few waterfall rivers in Arizona – most falls come from a creek!

Journal:

Date(s) Visited:

Weather
conditions:

Who you were with:

Nature observations:

Special memories:

Seven Falls

Located in the Bear Canyon and found at the Catalina Foothills, the falls are made up of limestone rocks. The hike to reach Seven Falls is one of the most popular trails in the Tucson region. This trail will take hikers to the beginning of the Seven Falls hike (Bear Canyon Trail). For those that do not want to hike, a tram can take visitors to the trailhead; this makes the trail only three to four miles rather than nine miles. The hike to reach Seven Falls will have hikers passing through rivers and creeks – it's best to wear water shoes during the trek. During the rainy season, the water to the falls can be waist-high. The waterfall is best to visit in the spring season when the water flow will be the most powerful. The limestone and granite rocks of the area offer vast colors and plants surrounding the falls. There are many small waterfalls during the high-flowing seasons, as the water forms pools at the falls' base. This is ideal for hikers looking to cool off after a day of hiking in the region, especially during the summer season when it's hot. The water flow in the area allows many plants to grow, unlike other Bear Canyon areas.

Best time to visit:
March to May
Pass/Permit/Fees:
$5 per vehicle
Closest city or town:
Tucson, Arizona
How to get there:
Fly or drive into Tucson and drive to the trailhead.
GPS Coordinates:
32.3273° N, 110.7702° W
Did You Know?
Exploring the region, you will find native cactus and even the Costa hummingbird, which is native to the area and Mexico.

Journal:

Date(s) Visited:

Weather conditions:

Who you were with:

Nature observations:

Special memories:

Ribbon Falls

Ribbon Falls is located within the Grand Canyon; it's the only waterfall in the park that can be reached without backpacking or rafting. The falls are located along the North Kaibab Trail or the Phantom Ranch Trail, and the trail mileage is about 12 to 16 miles round trip with an elevation change of 9,042 feet. The trek to reach Ribbon Falls can be very insane to any amateur hiker. *Chimik'yana'kya Deya'* is Ribbon Falls in Zuni, the language of the Native American Pueblo people who lived in the region. The falls are located 100 feet above the base of the pool and are full of rich minerals. Ribbon Falls is considered a sacred site for the Zuni people, believing this is where humans first emerged on the Earth. The Zuni people have a long history of living in the Grand Canyon region. Most people that hike to Ribbon Falls are part of a multi-day trip, as this is rarely a one-day trip given the intensity of the hike. The overhanging of the cliffs around the falls offers a great place to rest from the sun during the summer season. The water supply from the falls allows for vegetation in the small canyon to be lush compared to other areas of the Grand Canyon.

Best time to visit:
March to May, September to October
Pass/Permit/Fees:
Backcountry Camping Permit, $10 to $18 dollars a day
Closest city or town:
Tusayan, Arizona
How to get there:
Fly into Las Vegas, Salt Lake City, or Phoenix, and rent a car to drive to the Grand Canyon to start the hike.
GPS Coordinates:
37.7358° N, 119.6482° W
Did You Know?
There is a massive green travertine spire underneath the falls from mineral deposits!

Journal:

Date(s) Visited:

Weather conditions:

Who you were with:

Nature observations:

Special memories:

Pacheta Falls

Located in the Grand White Mountains, the Pacheta Falls are much less crowded than other famous falls in the state, making it popular among hikers that enjoy quiet and a more secluded hike. The waterfall is surrounded by rock formations and lush green vegetation due to the water! The falls stand over 131 feet high and have Douglas fir trees around – a sharp contrast to the average desert climate of Arizona. Unfortunately, swimming is not allowed at these falls; the rocks and water current are too dangerous. The hike to reach the falls is only 2.5 miles round trip, although a much longer car ride is needed to get to the trailhead – about two hours. Due to the waterfalls' isolated nature, it's very common to see wildlife, including elks, bears, and bighorn sheep. The falls are located on the White Mountain Apache Reservation and require a special permit to enter the area. The lack of cell phone service locating the falls can be problematic, and it's recommended to visit in the morning with ample sunlight. West of the falls is the meeting point of the three creeks in the area: the Spud, Ess, and Pacheta Creeks (which feeds the Pacheta Falls).

Best time to visit:
March to October
Pass/Permit/Fees:
Black River Special Use Permit, $15
Closest city or town:
Alpine, Arizona
How to get there:
Fly into Phoenix or Albuquerque airport and drive to the reservation and hiking trail.
GPS Coordinates:
33.6674° N, 109.5249° W
Did You Know?
This is one of the largest waterfalls and the most secluded in Arizona!

Journal:

Date(s) Visited:

Weather conditions:

Who you were with:

Nature observations:

Special memories:

Other Places

Place: _____

Date(s) visited:

Weather conditions:

Whom you were with:

Nature observations:

Special memories:

Place: _____

Date(s) visited:

Weather conditions:

Whom you were with:

Nature observations:

Special memories:

Place: _____

Date(s) visited:

Weather conditions:

Whom you were with:

Nature observations:

Special memories:

Place: _____

Date(s) visited:

Weather conditions:

Whom you were with:

Nature observations:

Special memories:

Place: _____

Date(s) visited:

Weather conditions:

Whom you were with:

Nature observations:

Special memories:

114

Place: _____

Date(s) visited:

Weather conditions:

Whom you were with:

Nature observations:

Special memories:

Place: _____

Date(s) visited:

Weather conditions:

Whom you were with:

Nature observations:

Special memories:

Place: _____

Date(s) visited:

Weather conditions:

Whom you were with:

Nature observations:

Special memories:

Place: _____

Date(s) visited:

Weather conditions:

Whom you were with:

Nature observations:

Special memories:

118

Place: _____

Date(s) visited:

Weather conditions:

Whom you were with:

Nature observations:

Special memories:

Credit the Incredible Photographers:

121

Salome Jug

http://2.bp.blogspot.com/_zudoIngEjsg/TUSRLHt4EII/AAAAAAAAAYU/Ls6FkUx-7-E/s1600/theJugfalls.JPG Salome Jug- Canyoneering [Exploring the Southwest: Salome Jug- Canyoneering]. (2011, January 29). Retrieved April 20, 2021, from http://hikingthesouthwest.blogspot.com/2011/01/salome-jug-canyoneering.html

Walnut Canyon

https://search.creativecommons.org/photos/8a94ba8c-ab45-4dd2-884c-80b4073c1d03

"Walnut Canyon" by sfbaywalk is licensed with CC BY 2.0. To view a copy of this license, visit https://creativecommons.org/licenses/by/2.0/

Wupatki National Monument

https://search.creativecommons.org/photos/cb712a4a-60c7-48de-b9ee-6b759553212a

"Wupatki Ruins Trail, Wupatki National Monument, Arizona" by Ken Lund is licensed with CC BY-SA 2.0. To view a copy of this license, visit https://creativecommons.org/licenses/by-sa/2.0/

Camelback Mountain

https://search.creativecommons.org/photos/6ec7c334-c604-48a4-a523-25c19618127b

"My Camelback Mountain End to End Hike" by Scot Rumery is licensed with CC BY-SA 2.0. To view a copy of this license, visit https://creativecommons.org/licenses/by-sa/2.0/

Mount Lemmon Scenic Byway

https://search.creativecommons.org/photos/b110fbaf-f595-4ce9-82c9-9934bb2722b4

"Mount Lemmon Trip" by 666isMONEY 🔘 ♥ & 🔧 is licensed with CC BY 2.0. To view a copy of this license, visit https://creativecommons.org/licenses/by/2.0/

Organ Pipe Cactus National Monument

https://search.creativecommons.org/photos/e74ec4b5-3e57-4776-9bb2-0bbe64668412

"Organ Pipe Cactus National Monument" by usareisetipps is licensed with CC BY-SA 2.0. To view a copy of this license, visit https://creativecommons.org/licenses/by-sa/2.0/

Kartchner Caverns

https://search.creativecommons.org/photos/f745f1c5-796b-466a-9e80-754889da1b2c

"File:A fault at Kartchner Caverns State Park..JPG" by Shaunnamm is licensed with CC BY-SA 4.0. To view a copy of this license, visit https://creativecommons.org/licenses/by-sa/4.0

Hoover Dam

https://search.creativecommons.org/photos/594d1452-a36e-4f03-bc70-19720b31c4d0

"The Hoover Dam" by M McBey is licensed with CC BY 2.0. To view a copy of this license, visit https://creativecommons.org/licenses/by/2.0/

Chiricahua National Monument

https://search.creativecommons.org/photos/a220bf26-ef2b-4819-8a59-a38008e6c55d

"Massai Point, Chiricahua National Monument, Arizona" by Ken Lund is licensed with CC BY-SA 2.0. To view a copy of this license, visit https://creativecommons.org/licenses/by-sa/2.0/

Coconino Lava River Cave

https://search.creativecommons.org/photos/2a2a2c29-35dc-4740-b7ba-260b1e50b446

"Lava River Cave Entrance" by Coconino NF Photography is marked under CC PDM 1.0. To view the terms, visit https://creativecommons.org/publicdomain/mark/1.0/

Desert Botanical Garden

https://search.creativecommons.org/photos/725f4ba4-4250-4f4f-85bf-831b6f63b631

"Desert Botanical Garden" by Artotem is licensed with CC BY 2.0. To view a copy of this license, visit https://creativecommons.org/licenses/by/2.0/

Vermilion Cliffs National Monument
https://search.creativecommons.org/photos/14be3975-1c6b-46d7-8c0a-bc9a05929533
"BLM Winter Bucket List #23: Vermilion Cliffs National Monument, Arizona, for Spectacular Geologic Features and Superbowl 49" by mypubliclands is licensed with CC BY 2.0. To view a copy of this license, visit https://creativecommons.org/licenses/by/2.0/

Humphreys Peak
https://search.creativecommons.org/photos/08243f1f-8cf0-4b48-bb26-055f48b1c2c5
"Humphreys Peak" by Coconino NF Photography is licensed with CC BY-SA 2.0. To view a copy of this license, visit https://creativecommons.org/licenses/by-sa/2.0/

Fossil Creek Falls
https://search.creativecommons.org/photos/5b66e342-6170-41c1-b83a-30927df15f24
"Waterfall Trail at Fossil Creek" by Coconino NF Photography is marked under CC PDM 1.0. To view the terms, visit https://creativecommons.org/publicdomain/mark/1.0/

Apache Falls
https://pixels.com/featured/2-apache-falls-jeff-swan.html
Swan, J. (2015, July 15). Apache Falls [Apache Falls in the Salt River Canyon in Arizona.]. Retrieved April 20, 2021, from https://pixels.com/featured/2-apache-falls-jeff-swan.html

Seven Falls
https://search.creativecommons.org/photos/998f7910-b752-4073-b02a-42003bb9049b
"Seven Falls, Tucson, Arizona" by Steven Gerner is licensed with CC BY-SA 2.0. To view a copy of this license, visit https://creativecommons.org/licenses/by-sa/2.0/

Ribbon Falls
https://search.creativecommons.org/photos/1996ef51-5f94-4114-bf02-6816b33e665a
"Grand Canyon National Park: Ribbon Falls 06940" by Grand Canyon NPS is licensed with CC BY 2.0. To view a copy of this license, visit https://creativecommons.org/licenses/by/2.0/

Pacheta Falls
https://c2.staticflickr.com/4/3060/2805252924_6c4367a4e8_b.jpg
Buff, R. (n.d.). Pacheta Falls [Digital image]. Retrieved April 20, 2021, from https://c2.staticflickr.com/4/3060/2805252924_6c4367a4e8_b.jpg

Cover photo: https://unsplash.com/photos/kg60TaG7RBk
Under Unsplash License – Photographer: Dave Herring

Made in the USA
Las Vegas, NV
23 May 2022

49250620R00069